EMOTIONAL LITERACY

Emotional Literacy

Collected Poems and Song Lyrics

ASH BROCKWELL

Reconnecting Rainbows

Emotional Literacy: Collected Poems and Song Lyrics
Dr Ash Brockwell, PhD
Published in the United Kingdom by Reconnecting Rainbows, an
imprint of Green Spiral Arts
First published in paperback in 2022
Printed and bound by Ingram Spark
ISBN 978-1-8383425-7-9

Reconnecting Rainbows is a collective of transgender and non-binary
writers, illustrators, and publishers in the UK and internationally.

For more information or to enquire about commercial use of this
material, please visit www.reconnectingrainbows.co.uk

CONTENTS

Empathy

Shame, Pride, Both?

Confusion

Desperation

Inner Conflict

Yearning

Joy

Hope

Unrequited Love, Season 2

Loneliness

Heartbreak

Self-Love

Acceptance

Gratitude

Courage

Excitement

Pride

Euphoria

Fear

Frustration

Defiance

Exasperation

...laugh, leaning back in my arms
for life's not a paragraph
And death i think is no parenthesis

                      - e. e. cummings

Emotional Literacy

You're trying to tell me
LIFE IS NOT A PARAGRAPH.

Darling, I'm sorry, I didn't mean to laugh,
but I've been addicted to words since I was, oh, let me think,
approximately one and a half.

I don't remember it but my mother used to tell me
how she'd wheel me in my pushchair round the shop
and I'd yell for her to stop
and let me read the labels on the tins:
Ma-ca-ro-ni.
Man-da-rins.

Those were the golden days. I didn't dream
that at four they'd start me off
on the Rainbow Reading Scheme.
See you. See me. I am a tree. How twee. I'd hide
in the Big School's library and lose myself in rhyme.
I remember how I cried
when I found a poem about the slipping away of time,
and again when I was told,
at seven and a quarter, I was millions of seconds old.

At eight (new school) they gave me *Pride and Prejudice*.
Give them credit. Well, they tried,
but what does an eight-year-old know of prejudice or pride?

At ten I announced I was inspired.
I acquired a magic panda who would chew
metaphysical questions and imaginary fresh bamboo.
I chronicled her exploits with a kid of ten
(oddly like me, with spectacles, and hair in bunches)
and sent them off to publishers.
Of course, they were rejected.
It was no more or less than I expected.
For what does an eleven-year-old
(as I must have been by then)
know about agents and Litter-airy Lunches?

I didn't care. I always got a personal letter,
and all the handbooks told me not to expect much better.
I didn't realise that even publishers couldn't be so cruel
as to send a standard rejection slip c/o primary school.

And after all these years?

Well, it appears
that I've moved on from *look at me I am a tree*
to *look at me*
I am the sum total of the neurochemical synaptic potentials
of my left and right cerebral hemispheres.

Life is not a paragraph.
That's a quotation, in case you didn't know it.
I could give you a potted biography of the poet.
I could direct you to the book:
shop on the corner, first floor,
second row, third shelf.
In fact, I could probably tell you more about the book
than I could about myself.

Life is not a paragraph?
Darling, do you think you could possibly visit
when you've a minute? you see, I've lost my library ticket,
and I'm dying to find out:
if it isn't a paragraph,
then what,
exactly,
is it?

BACK STORY

Somehow, it's forty years since I wrote my first poem, *Valentine's Day*. I've written a lot of poems and song lyrics over those four decades, but *Emotional Literacy* – written in my late teens, when I was an undergraduate at Oxford in the 1990s – is still my favourite. It was inspired by graffiti. On a brick wall in Parks Road, which I walked past every day on my way to the biochemistry building, someone spray-painted the words 'LIFE IS NOT A PARAGRAPH' in bold white capitals. I recognised them as a misquotation from a poem by e. e. cummings that I'd read the previous week (it's on page xi, after the table of contents, if you missed it) and they resonated strongly with me.

Everything in the poem is true, although the 'Darling' addressed in it was not a real person: at least, I didn't have anyone specific in mind when I wrote it. Aside from a short-lived relationship with my lab partner in the summer of my first year, I was single throughout my undergraduate course. This was the result of a fierce inner conflict between my enthusiasm for religion, which I had embraced that same summer after being 'converted' by a fellow student, and the realisation that I was queer. I didn't have any words to articulate it: all I knew was that I was clearly something *other* than a woman who was attracted exclusively to men. 'Bisexual' was my best guess at the time (it was much later in life that I settled on 'non-binary transmasculine'). Yet my chosen faith community was adamant: there were men and there were women, and the only acceptable type of relationship involved one of each.

The 'Darling' in *Emotional Literacy* could have been a premonition of Loni, the best friend I met at the start of my second year, who did a wonderful job of showing me the joys of a life beyond books. With our mutual friend and partner in crime, Pinku, we found our bliss in unexpected places – late-night blues music with midnight feasts of cheesy chips, impromptu expeditions to distribute leftover Christmas pudding to homeless people (as documented in the poem *Flipflops in December*), encaustic painting, picnics by the river, and a public performance of our co-written nonsense poetry. In a mixture of real and invented words, we poked fun at the conservative Oxford establishment and its archaic language, from the 'Bod' (Bodleian Library) to the 'Quad' or quadrangle, the neatly manicured square of grass in the centre of our college courtyard, upon which even professors were forbidden to walk.

Life was certainly much more than a paragraph with Loni and Pinku around. It was thanks to them that I survived at all. My radical, creative, *feeling* side had to be suppressed temporarily – trapped in a bottle like Aladdin's genie – while I spent the better part of my day alone in the lab, masked and gloved, pipetting liquids into plastic bottles of pancreatic cells. But in the evenings, with them, I came back to life.

The inner conflict intensified when, in my fourth and final year, I realised I had fallen in love with Loni. She was a singer, poet, traveller, and mystic - unconventional in every way, and yet somehow, inexplicably, heterosexual. She rejected my clumsy advances and laughed at me. While this wasn't the sole cause, it was a key factor in my decision to accept an internship in Tanzania – helping to organise an international conference on herbal remedies for malaria – as soon as my written exams were over. I didn't even wait to see if I had a viva, which might have enabled me to upgrade my 2:1 to a first-class degree.

On one level, exchanging the biochemistry lab for the slopes of Mount Meru was the best thing I had ever done. I found myself welcomed by a loving and supportive community that was unlike anything I had ever experienced before. At first, with all the naïve optimism of the very young and privileged, I felt as though I had stepped into a magical universe of sunshine, flowers and music, where anything was possible. Within weeks, I had fallen for the charms of a young Tanzanian writer, written a new batch of poems, and thrown in my lot with a group of artist-activists who wanted to start an organisation to preserve Indigenous arts and culture.

The short version is that I came to Tanzania for six months and stayed for ten years, although the reality was messier and more complicated than that. Of course, the novelty wore off, as novelty always does; but it was several years before it fully sank in that I had stepped out of one set of unwritten rules and into another. Caught up in the excitement of starting project after project, I barely noticed that I was getting trapped in new social roles: fiancée, wife, mother, safari company CEO, 'Woman of the Year' finalist (I know, ironic, right?!) and self-appointed white saviour. Whatever I tried to do, there was always a fine line between admiration and ridicule. Worse, I was so exhausted from trying to learn all the parts at once that I had no sense of who I really *was*, when I wasn't performing.

It all started to unravel in 2009 when the global financial crash destroyed the budget and mid-range safari market – and in the same year, my marriage fell apart. By May 2010, I was back in the UK with my two young daughters, then seven and four, as a single parent. I was in pieces - simultaneously grieving the loss of my marriage, my business, my religious community, my entire circle of friends, and all the roles that I'd grown used to playing. I'd left my lovely house on the outskirts of Arusha, with its garden full of mango trees, monkeys, and sunbirds, to live in a damp, windowless room in my parents' basement. I was battling reverse culture shock, which proved far worse than the initial culture shock of going to Tanzania in the first place. Worst of all, the city where I'd managed to land a part-time research job turned out to be the country's gay capital. After so many years of denial, it came as a shock to find myself surrounded by very 'out' and visible LGBTQ+ people. As I wrote in the poem *In All The Places: 'In all the places I could have ended up / I ended up here, in the city of rainbow flags / The irony was, I never even knew.'*

The conflict between my religion and my queerness came to a head in 2012, taking me to some very dark places – as documented in *A Queer Love/Hate Poem to God*. The fact that I survived to tell the tale is largely thanks to a business card that I picked up in a café in Brighton, advertising 'spiritual counselling'. My therapist gently helped me to question whether I really believed the hard-line religious position, encouraging me to make art as a way of accessing deeper levels of understanding. She directed me to *The Artist's Way* by Julia Cameron, a course in overcoming creative blocks, as well as to a book on co-dependency that transformed my relationships with my family. Within weeks, I was painting as though my life depended on it. (It probably did.) By 2013 I had a joint exhibition with another artist at a local gallery.

A few days before my thirty-ninth birthday I resigned from what was meant to be a permanent job as a researcher, abandoned the religious movement that I'd belonged to for over twenty years, and came out as a lesbian to my entire circle of

Facebook friends. These three major life changes were all inter-related, in that my boss and some of my colleagues also belonged to the same homophobic religion. The pressure of trying to play the role of what I later called 'The Person I Thought They Wanted Me To Be', or The PITTWAM-2B for short, was breaking me from the inside - and I knew it. At the time, I thought my attraction to women was the main issue – although, for reasons that I couldn't fathom, I was never fully comfortable with the label of 'lesbian'. It wasn't until 2017 that I discovered the language of non-binary gender and realised what had been the issue all along: *I wasn't a woman.*

Coming out as transgender proved to be a very different experience from coming out as a lesbian. Some of the people who had been supportive or unfazed by my revelations about my sexuality now thought I had lost my mind. But with support from a new partner who was also transitioning (albeit in the opposite direction), I realised that the 'bleurgh' feeling that I had been carrying around all my life – a deep sense of being wrong, not enough, and a failure as a woman – was gender dysphoria. As I learned to navigate chest-binding, new clothes, a new hair-cut, a new legal name, and eventually hormone treatment, I started to experience the opposite emotion: *gender euphoria.* My new-found happiness was marred only by the realisation of how much hatred and abuse the trans community faces, both in the media and on the streets. While my partner and I didn't experience anything worse than verbal harassment, we knew plenty of people who had been physically attacked.

There's much more I could say about the back story, and maybe one day I'll write a full autobiography; but for now, I want to let the poems and lyrics speak for themselves. The works in this volume span four decades, from *Valentine's Day* in 1982 to *Free Speech* in 2022. They're arranged chronologically, with a few exceptions. In places, I've grouped poems from different eras together around a similar emotional theme, and there are also some – especially in the early part of the book – that were written retrospectively. *Misfit* and *Flipflops in December,* for example, belonged to a collection that I wrote between 2016 and 2017, along with all the 'Unrequited Love: Season 2' poems. I had been hoping to publish this very small collection with the title *The Only Thing In All The Universe That I Can Never Tell You,* but life got in the way and I never found the time.

The five *Songs of the Gathering,* also written in 2017, have been separated out at the end to make it easier to find them. I'm in the process of writing a non-fiction book around these songs. They frame a process that I call the 'TLC Gathering', short for 'Talking, Listening, and Co-Creating', which I've been trying out in different settings – song circles in my living room, online gatherings via Zoom, and even a live workshop at the national conference of the British Ecological Society. But before I can write convincingly about this process, I want to test it out more extensively with leaders and educators within the environmental activism and regenerative design movements. I'm also hoping to use it to build collective mental wellbeing and resilience in other settings (including the trans and non-binary community). If the songs resonate with you, please feel free to sing them to any tunes that you can find or make up, and to use them in TLC Gatherings of your own.

It's been fun putting this collection together, revisiting memories from the past four decades, and trying to categorise them all according to the predominant emotion. My writing buddy, whose own emotional literacy is evidently a lot better than mine, was very patient with my annoying questions along the lines of 'Is X an emotion?' (the answer was usually no!) and did an excellent job of helping me find the right heading for the right poem. There was only one poem that utterly resisted all efforts to attach a singular emotion to it: *A Lover's Guide to the Electromagnetic Spectrum*. As it's one of my favourites, I didn't want to leave it out, so I decided to give it the heading of 'The Entire Emotional Roller-Coaster'.

In re-reading, organising, and editing all these poems, I finally found an answer to the twenty-year-old mystery: the identity of the 'Darling' in *Emotional Literacy*. If this were a Hollywood movie, I'd have reconnected with at least one of the former objects of my unrequited affection through the process of compiling the book, and they'd have fallen deeply in love with the transmasculine version of me. The reality was more prosaic, but at the same time, more satisfying. I recognised the subject of the poem as the one person who's been there through every single one of these changing moods: ME! When the 18-year-old me asked wistfully, 'Darling, do you think you could possibly visit / when you've a minute?', the response that came back was from my own brave, creative, soulful side – my inner muse who refused to be content with a paragraph.

I hope you enjoy reading about my (ongoing) journey towards emotional literacy, and that it helps you to recognise your own inner muse when they show up in your life.

Love and solidarity,

Dr Ash Brockwell (he/him), August 2022

A NOTE ABOUT TRIGGER WARNINGS

If you are a trauma survivor, you're advised to read this book with caution and avoid sections with headings like 'Desperation' or 'Heartbreak' on days when you're already struggling.

When a poem makes an explicit reference to suicidal thoughts, the heading itself includes a trigger warning. There are only three of these. *Surviving (But Only Just)* also contains self-harm references, and the poems *Sometimes Waving but Mostly Drowning* and *Free Speech* also contain references to transphobic hate crime.

CURIOSITY AND WONDER

A collection of poems from my early childhood

Valentine's Day
(Age 4)

Today is Valentine's Day,
With puddles in the street,
And ladies with umbrellas,
And welly-booted feet!

Bonfire Night
(Age 5)

What we have on bonfire night
Is a guy and a bonfire burning bright
Pretty fireworks go on and on
Until the bonfire night is gone.
Sparklers, rockets flying high,
Bangs on the pavement,
Bangs in the sky.

Oak Tree
(Age 7)

You grew from an acorn
That I myself planted.
I had you indoors, and you became my friend.
You grew to a seedling,
Then you grew to a sapling.
You grew to a tree. You were a tree.
Now you bear acorns,
and I plant them,
Hoping to get another friend like you.

TEENAGE ANGST

Psychobabble (Age 15)

I'm so glad you're ready to make a new start:
Please free your emotions and pour out your heart,
Release all your feelings through drama and art,
And then you can conquer your fears...
Now, some of your memories may be repressed,
Write down all the feelings you've never expressed -
I know it'll hurt, but it's all for the best...
No exit until you're in tears!

You seem to be coping! I'll give you a tip:
Forget the brave face and the stiff upper lip...
'The older the shoulder, the bigger the chip'
Should be your new motto, it's clear.
The happy man's no more advanced than a chimp,
Our modern society favours the wimp,
And sympathy goes to the listless and limp:
We don't want your smiles in here!

Don't bottle up anger, just let it all out,
It's OK to scream and to throw things about,
And most things are cured by a jolly good shout –
But come back next week without fail!
On this point, dear client, I must be emphatic
(Attendance till now has been rather erratic...)
You really need help when your life's so traumatic -
I'm sorry you've broken your nail.

DESIRE

How Not To Experiment With A Chemist

A scientist investigating sexual attraction
Decided he was bored with being left upon the shelf,
And so, convinced that love was just a chemical reaction,
He thought the only answer was to make the stuff himself.
With Inorganic all he got was salt, or some such mess –
Organic seemed more hopeful, so he turned to that instead.
A radical decision, but it brought him no success,
For benzene rings are not the kind that help to get you wed.
(At first he thought that ethanol might hold the key to sex,
But this illusion faded when he tested its effects).

As things were not proceeding at a very steady rate,
He found himself a catalyst, whose name was Molly Bdenum,
And when they shared a Bunsen, well, she got in such a state
He figured that eventually, they'd work it out between 'em.
The heat was on, the pressure high, and then it happened fast:
Experiments had started getting physical at last!

When things were getting steamy (or at least a little heated)
He set up his spectrometer and did the calibration –
Then Molly started moaning
at the way that she'd been treated,
And suddenly exploded at his lack of concentration.
The insults that she flung at him whilst heading for the door
Were as painful and as sour as his H_2SO_4.

As he tried to find an order in the chaos and confusion,
And find out what had happened
to the feeling that he treasured,
The mechanism struck him and he came to this conclusion:
It's just a basic instinct and its pH can't be measured.

Author's Note:

I wrote this poem in my A-level Chemistry class and
pinned it up on the college noticeboard. I wasn't
quite brave enough to put my name on it, though,
so I signed it 'X. Periment' instead!)

UNREQUITED LOVE, SEASON 1

Misfit

I never understood the posters, the crushes,
the dates, the dances. Never got it. Something was wrong
with me, even then, but I never knew what.
Where was my desire: why didn't my heart beat faster?
And then at last I met you, and I understood.
You're a straight girl. I'm ~&1*63#(.
This is a disaster.

Author's Note:

These symbols, from the code that I made up with
my childhood best friend when we were both ten,
translate as 'bisexual'. This was exactly how I wrote
the word in my journal, a full decade later, for fear
that someone would find it and read it! In hindsight,
'bisexual' didn't make sense, as I wasn't attracted to
men – only women – but it felt like a safer place to
start than 'lesbian' or 'queer'. At the time, I'd never
even heard the word 'transgender', let alone 'non-
binary'.

Flipflops in December

You always had to be different.
Flipflops in December:
not a warm African December, but an Oxford one,
with cold grey pavements under a cold grey sky,
and people who gave cold grey stares. You didn't
care (my Loni my love my dearest heart
whose official title was *friend*).
singing the blues at 1am
chips and cheese at 2am
crazy poems at 3am
you brought me alive
from the inside out
my Loni my love
(but I never told you that)

You always had to be different. Feeding the homeless
with Christmas pudding while my parents were waiting
in the car to take me home for Christmas.
Who knows what the homeless thought, but my parents
were furious. It was the first time
I hadn't put them first; the first time I'd almost
forgotten they existed. When I was with you,
I forgot the world (my Loni my precious my sweetest love
whose official title was *friend*)

essay crisis at 4am
losing the plot at 5am
falling asleep at 6am

I sleepwalked through life
until the day I met you
my Loni my love
(but I never told you that)

You always had to be different. Telling a Muslim friend
he'd have to marry us both, and we'd become
his 'awful wedded wives'. Forget the love triangle; I
would have been happy with two sides
of an equation, you plus me. We could have been
each other's wives instead,
if only you'd loved me like I loved you.
But it wasn't to be.

It would have been awful.
I know that now.
I might not have survived
for long as your wife,
even if you'd loved me. But still
I could dream (my Loni my darling
my secret desire
whose official title was *friend*).

CONTENTMENT

Savannah Song

Swim with me through a sea of yellowed grass:
the vastness of the empty plains will be our guide.
Ride with me on a zebra's back
across the land of endless space:
a place to dream, and free our souls
from all the clutter that we left behind inside.
Step by step, side by side, shaking the gravel from our shoes:
stopping to talk with all we meet, for there is time
to gain, to grow in wisdom and in faith,
not time to lose.

Mamas are waiting to welcome us with love and tea:
Seeing through smoke and dust, we gladly drink our share.
There in the heart of savannah let us sit and talk a while,
smile, and laugh,
and share the smoky yogurt mixed with maize.
These are the days to dream, and know we are alive.

We arrive at sunset, as the cows come home,
their bells chiming to welcome us to our place of rest.
Blessed by the setting sun, and by the fathers of the land,
we understand the reasons for the long and dusty trail.
And we may fail, and fall, and cry; but rise again, and walk,
And know that love is endless, and our spirits whole.

Author's Note:

Both the electronic files and the hard copies of the
poems that I wrote in Tanzania in 2000-2010 were
lost during successive moves. *Savannah Song* has
been reconstructed from memory: I think the original version had another verse, but I can't remember
it now. To avoid reinforcing stereotypes, I want to
make it very clear that I lived in a modern, cos-
mopolitan city, in a house with electricity, running
water and internet access. Village visits like this one
were a regular feature of my experience, but not the
entirety of it. My life, and the people I loved, were
often misrepresented in the media – and this poem
could easily be used in the same way. I've included
it only because I didn't want to skip over an entire
decade.

EMPATHY

Reverse Culture Shock

I have learnt to call my homeland 'home' again:
To buy cheese knives, lemon slicers and sweetcorn forks;
To look down at the ground, and never talk to strangers;
To be grateful for sun, and curse the dreary rain;
To forget to be amazed by autumn trees;
To keep my children indoors, earphones in ears;
To wear black (it goes with everything), and carry a coat;
To run for the bus (it won't reverse to meet me).
To pay with my left hand, without any guilt;
To sleep with no net, and wake with no need to scratch;
To shop in supermarkets without overwhelm;
To turn on a tap, and not jump if the water's hot;
But I don't think I'll ever learn to stop saying polé.

Polé. We don't have this word.
The closest we come is 'sorry',
But 'sorry' implies blame, or shame.
'Sorry' says "it was me."
Polé: "it's not my fault, but I see your pain.
I hope this gets better soon. I empathise.
May the heat become less." It's meaningless in the cold,

But I say it anyway. It's wired into my brain,
when somebody coughs or stumbles, cries or falls,
breaks a leg, feels tired, becomes bereaved,
loses their job, loses their dog, or loses their way.
For the English, somehow, there's only an awkward gap
where polé should be. A shuffle: a muttered "Oh dear,
are you all right?" (when the answer is clearly 'no');
a wordless hug, or a stiff-upper-lip-old-chap.

Author's Note:

'Polé' is a Swahili word and there are no acute
accents in written Swahili, but I've added one as an
indication that the word is pronounced 'POH-lay',
not 'pole' as in the North Pole.

SHAME, PRIDE, BOTH?

Of All The Places

Of all the places I could have ended up,
I ended up here, in the city of rainbow flags.
The irony is, I never even knew.
So closeted, so closed, I had no clue
what the flags even meant. I had no idea at all.

So not only do I pick up a book and read my own story in it
And not only do I watch TV and see my life reflected back
And not only do I listen to the song
asking 'how is this wrong?'
But I'm also faced with the flags
and the banners and the posters
and the Pride marches and the LGBT History Month
and the buses saying SOME PEOPLE ARE GAY,
GET OVER IT!
and the flyers and the newsletters
and the e-mails about Pink Fringe
and the gay village maps and the G3 magazines in Starbucks
and every day I walk down that corridor and see that poster
advertising the Lesbian Lives Conference.

There's nowhere to hide here.

And I dream of a quiet life in a quiet place
where I never hear these words again.

But then strange things happen:
A small voice says yes to the rainbow.
(Although another shouts NO!)

Their arguments in my head are killing me slowly,
But the *Yes* is getting louder.
There's no way back.

CONFUSION

On the Imprisonment of LGBTQ+ Rights Campaigners

some people are jailed
because they demand the right
to make love

some people are elected
because they demand the right
to make war

I'm a bit confused

tell me again
why it isn't the
other way around?

DESPERATION

A Queer Love/Hate Poem to God

It's thanks to you that I'm alive.
I hate you more with every day.
You almost make me want to die.
I love you more than words can say.

I want to smash your godly face,
but all I do is punch the air.
I want to feel your soft embrace,
but when I sleep there's no-one there.

I want to burn the Holy Book
and throw the ashes in the sea,
But even if I burned the world,
I'd breathe the smoke and there you'd be.

You pin me up against a wall.
There's no way out. There's no way through.
I want to, but I can't. I won't.
I'm leaving her. I'm leaving you.

I can't forget. I can't remember.
Have to. Can't. I won't give in.
I need to. Can't, though. There's no path.
It never works. I just can't win.

So why the hell did you create
a creature wired up all wrong?
I love her. Hate her. Love you. Hate you.
Love that girl and hate this song.

You made my heart. You made the rules.
So what the fuck? Why don't they match?
You tell me love is good. I love her.
What's so bad, then? Where's the catch?

You tell me, "Pray." I've prayed and prayed
until I thought my soul would crack.
Why don't you listen? Can't you hear?
There's no way forward, no way back.

I wish I'd never heard her name.
I wish I'd never heard your voice,
Then I could love her all my life.
I wish I didn't have this choice.

It's thanks to you I want to die.
I hate you more than words can say.
You almost make me feel alive.
I love you more with every day.

INNER CONFLICT

cover me in concrete

cover me in concrete and I'll still break through
brick me up and I'll grow through the cracks
you've always denied me, tried to hide me,
told me, *no, sorry,*
I'm not going to dance to that rhythm,
you can get lost

close your eyes but the tears still flow
lock me in but I'll still burst out
you've refused to name me, tried to shame me,
told me, *no way, no chance,*
that's not who I am,
now go away and leave me alone

but I'm deeper than you think and I'm going nowhere
I'm the tingle in your body that makes you glow
I'm the thrill of desire and forbidden love
and you know, oh, you know how you want to possess me
bless me, caress me, with all your heart...

no, for God's sake shut up,
I told you I didn't want to hear it
and I still don't, OK??

you can't stop me now that I'm back in control
I'm a part of your soul, your light, your dreams
I'm the voice that screams in the night: let me out!
and you'll have no peace till you finally quit
the pretence of a life that doesn't make sense
and admit what you never meant to admit
I can hear your heart and it's growing stronger
fears from the past can't last much longer
let me out and I'll set you free
let me out and you'll finally be
the person you always yearned to be
let me out and you won't regret it...

NO DAMN WAY! I SAID FORGET IT!
I'm doing fine, I'm happy in here,
this life is safe, the path is clear...

I'm sorry, my love, I have to insist:
you're dancing to my rhythm now, you can't resist

ok, you win, I'm not really happy, it's all a lie...
but I can say this only once, and only very quietly,
and only if you're sure nobody's listening,
and only if you swear
not to tell a soul.
promise?
are you sure?

Yes, I loved her.
Yes, I dreamed of her.
Yes, I desired her.
Yes, I grieved for her.

Oh my God, what did I just say???
CANCEL
DELETE
ESCAPE

Who, me?
No, I didn't say anything.
Nothing at all.

YEARNING

Spring Equinox, Avebury

Don't tell me you can't feel it: the ache within,
that yearns to begin again where you might begin,
to ride out, unafraid, to the origin; to honour your Goddess.
To breathe deep of the honest air, unconditioned: breathe,
and receive life in every cell,
as your blood resounds with hope.
There is hope in the ancient stones, carved with devoted love,
and your fingers long to caress their contours, connect
to the ley lines of your own ancestral lands.

Desire, it is Love I desire: no mere body, but Love,
and Love in the body, and soul, and blossom; Love
in the chalk-white path, and the crows,
and the soft-curved hill.
and the sparkling eyes of the man in the tattered clothes,
who carves the ancient yew
and crafts his stones into stories.
It's true: I've dreamed them all.
I've heard the cry of those crows.

I've pressed a coin into that wrinkled hand.
I've walked that path before. I understand.
I AM this land, and this land is Me,
and all that you said is real...
I feel...

...But enough of this! Get out of my life! I have to work.
(It costs too much to breathe that air,
which vibrates with all I've lost.)
I'd prefer it if you left.
Go and walk your chalk, or fly with crows,
or chase those rainbow dreams, or carve your yew,
or do whatever the hell it was that you wanted me to do.
Believing in stones and bones: what are you, a shaman?
Please, just GO...

Hello? Security?
Yes, I'd like to report an intruder in my heart -
Sorry, I meant my office... Can you still hear me?
Are you there?

You needn't call security. I'll leave quietly now, dear heart.
It isn't about belief. Believe in the air, if you will,
or refuse to believe; but bodies breathe, all the same,
and the air might come alive
on the day when you learn your name.

Hunched at your desk, you never saw the rainbow. But love
is not grasping; love is not clutching. Love is only surrender.
Butterflies die in a tight-clenched fist,
however warm and tender.

I'm here if you need me, beloved, and the Avebury stones
have stood three thousand years:
I can wait a few years longer.

No more rhyme, no more reason.
The four vast birches are calling.
The moss, diamond-wet, is calling out to my toes.

JOY

Beltane

Even if there is never anything else
there will always be today:
exquisite white flowers of may
and green morning-glow leaves of oak
sundancing the mysteries of May
to inquisitive birds, and beyond them to the bluest
(true dream) of skies, and unseen breeze.

My Goddess, my beloved,
and I, your pilgrim: we walk
in reverence and heart-core love
through your hidden temple, unknown
to human devotees. I touch
my cheek to the oak's rough bark,
feel the strength of its years within me:
caress the softness of moss, growing damp
with silent ecstasy; touch the hawthorn leaf
to my lips, and whisper wordless joy: I am alive!

"May I?" a tentative whisper. The response: I may.
A delicate sprig of may-blossom yields to my touch,
slips into my waiting hand. I hold her, more gently
than I can bear: tonight we will dance
in the liquid silver of full moon, and give thanks.

If there is nothing else in my life
there will always be this pure moment of forever
when my darling calls me *darling*, and my Goddess vows
to love all of me for all time (whether this earthly echo
resounds and grows louder, or fades and dissolves
in autumn rains and falls silent).

If love must pass away
into the winter tomb (womb) I will grieve for a season,
but spring will return to restore me.
She (with a capital S) is deathless, changeless;
she (with a small s) cares for me,
deeply and indisputably, for today.

May we? Only She knows.
Perhaps we may.

HOPE

Imbolc (First Stirrings of Spring)

there's a softening within, where I never knew
how much I had hardened; something stirs in me:
not a springtime flood at the surface, but a soft
whisper of loveblood flowing though calcified veins.

open me up with your touch (my love) let me breathe
deeper than lungs knew how, and let me dive in
to the inner core of soul that nobody entered before.
(darling) let me melt into you, all resistance gone,
and speak in tones that affirm the resurgence of hope.

my Goddess of the sacred spring, relight the flame,
stretch out the days with your heartwarm hands, and let
me dream once more; let new possibilities sprout
like snowdrops victorious over the frozen earth,
deceptively delicate, symbols of inner strength.

UNREQUITED LOVE, SEASON 2

The Only Thing In The Universe That I Can't Tell You

I told you all my secrets
the embarrassing ones and the precious ones
and you kept them all

I told you all my dreams
the wild ones and the hilarious ones
and you honoured them all

I told you the innermost joys of my heart
I told you where I came from and where I want to go
I told you what brings me alive
and you brought me alive
even more than before

there is only one thing left to say
the one thing I can't ever say to you
because the last person I said it to
freaked out and disappeared
from my life for ever
(and I can't risk that)

the only thing in the entire universe
that I can't tell you
is this (darling) I'm
in love
with
you

so the irony is
that you are the last person in the entire universe
I would share this book with
even though I want to more than anything
because I know that you are not
and whatever I do
never will be
in love
with
me

Surfsearching

what is it that I surfsearch for
night after night when the house is quiet
and everyone is in bed, keeping my secrets
inprivatebrowsing and password protected?

whatever it is
I could have found it in the hand that I held
(caressing it exquisitely between both of mine)
I could have found it if only

what is it that I long to read
squeezed into the spaces between gay clubs
and book clubs and anti-valentine speed dating
and older lgbTEA?

whatever it is
I could have read it in meltingchocolate eyes
(that struggled to say something words never will)
I could have read it if only

I don't have the words to whisper in your ear
(even if your ear were close enough)
I don't have the rainbow flag to wave
(mydarling) I don't know where to begin
(if only he hadn't found you first)
(if only you didn't prefer cis men)
(if only the heartbeats that almost rupture my veins
had the same effect on yours) (if only you
would touch me just one more time and be touched
by the power that sets me ablaze) (if only

Catch The Words

I have to catch the words on my tongue *beloved*
trap them behind my teeth before they slip out *my love*
stay strong, build the walls higher *my darling*
so I don't say it don't say it don't say it *I love you*

I have to sit on my hands so they don't reach out for yours
I have to buckle in my lips so they don't brush yours
lock it away, numb the pain, the joy and everything with it

hold myself up, hold myself in, hold myself together
so I don't touch don't touch don't touch *I need to hold you*

I let you come too close just once and you melted me
liquefied me into a flowing stream of hope/desire
then walked away unknowing and left me nameless,
wordless, helpless, rootless like a fragile seedling
ripped too early from the earth *come back to me*

don't leave my heart open and weeping: tell me the truth
if you never wanted to be with me, or never thought of love;
or else taste me *my precious* breathe me *my only* call to me
through the vastness of space *my healer*
where we met each other before time and until times run dry
my Goddess my beloved my heart's desire
my mystery my vision
my soulmemory
my dreamscape
my peace

Living On Borrowed Time

these moments of mine
when (if only in my heart) we both belong
only to each other and to the Infinite One
are not grand gestures but simple moments of peace:

lying still on a cliff top in spring sunshine and watching
the soft in-and-out breath of your silhouette
against the blue sky. releasing my tension
and fear in the calm accepting love of your arms.

watching you cut cabbage, slice beetroot,
scatter berries, with a deep sense of joy, an it's-all-
going-to-be-fine-ness that puts up two fingers
to the figures on statements (yes, I borrowed the fare
from the bank; borrowed the time from my job
and my family; all just to borrow you
for a few snatched hours). with you, I breathe free,
the chains around me loosen; you lift the weight
of the world's expectations. you expect nothing
from me, except to be present: to hold you when
you cry, to see you strong and wise and beautiful on the days
when you feel swamped in never-quite-enough-ness:

which, by the way, is effortless for me
because I don't know if you know
but even in your weakest hour
I only ever see you strong and wise
and beautiful and enough
(so much more than enough)

(if I could only have all of you it would be enough
for all of me for all time...but no! I mustn't think that way...)

these moments (not `stolen', but borrowed) are enough
to water my fragile seedlings of opening-up-to-love-ness,
echo back my first whispers of believing-in-myself-ness,
fan the flame of my half-daring-to-dream-ness,
reflect my faint glimmer of completeness.
incredible, isn't it, that a woman,
merely by being who she is, can do so much?

when you leave I will have to water my seedlings myself;
echo my own truth, fan my own flames, reflect my light
in my own mirror (somehow).

but meanwhile nobody can repossess these times
from me or from you; never ever
(under my breath: *beloved*) never ever

Before you go

There's a nuclear missile aiming right at my heart,
counting down seconds; and none of the action men
in Hollywood's greatest movies will ever be able to stop
this apocalypse. I want to freeze time, hit pause, just hold
myself forever in this frame: the moment before you go.

I was never good at goodbyes. Remember Lady Macbeth:
'Tis well if 'twere done quickly. Please get it over now:
don't leave me clinging on like a homeless ghost,
dreaming of waking from endless midsummer nights
to find the truth-of-your-going gone, or never waking
at all, or waking forgetting I loved you. (Dream on.)

I'll stop mixing my metaphors now. Let's keep things short
and not-at-all-sweet. **OK, bye.** Shut the door when you go.
Shut the door to the heart that you opened; I'll lock it
behind you. Oh, fuck it, there's not much point
in shutting the door: you've smashed the entire wall. It took
me years to construct. I'll have to start all over again: rebuild
my defences. I can't afford to live like this, tender
and trembling. I'm not that type. I'll always be tough.

but then there's another part of me
that yearns to gift you my tears
and sing you the song from the core of my soul
that explains exactly how
your warmth has kindled my blood, and how your love
(even the crumbs that fell
from your partner's plate) has sublimed my life;
and meld to you one last time,
and swim in the agony/ecstasy of your touch, and fling myself
into the heart of the fire of my liquefied heart
(beloved) till I and breath and my worthless words
evaporate, and leave no trace of a trace....

LONELINESS

October

October is the hardest and most beautiful time
when everything is calling me to let go and release
and the scarlet crimson gold ember-glow-orange
sienna of fallen leaves fills me with wonder
at the magic of transformation that turns
whatever no longer serves us
into compost for the new
and yet still the letting-go and releasing
leaves a bare space on the branch
and there is still a chiming bell
somewhere in the distance
reminding me
I fight back against the urge to say
'reminding me I am still alone'
because I know I am never
ever truly alone
yet still there
is that bare
space

HEARTBREAK

Metamorphosis

the breaking of the heart
is not a shattering into fragments,
not a forever destruction; but a process of sprouting,
a cracking of hardened shell. just as
water germinates seed, so too do tears
moisten and dissolve whatever solidified
within us, making a tiny tender place
where new growth can begin.

if I had never met you, I wouldn't
have known this pain. that much
is true. but if I had never met you, I
would be someone else: still ruled by fear,
afraid to love or trust, still living small.

you lifted me up and led me to
a threshold. from my deepest heart
I thank you for that, even though it's
the threshold of darkness.

your love
has changed me from caterpillar
to pupa, and here within this dark cocoon
a more profound change will begin.

I have no idea who I am
in this chrysalis. all I thought I knew
has dissolved. the things that felt simple
and safe now feel like chains. the old
structures must break down first, before the new
can form. I learnt to love again, and trust
again: now comes the harder task of
learning what to do with a newly
opened heart.

there's no way back: the
caterpillar body is gone.
all I can do
is wait in the darkness, holding to nothing
but trust and love, and know
that (cell by cell, and silently, and in ways
I can't see) through the grief and the pain
my rainbow wings will take shape
and I
will
fly.

SELF-LOVE

Even Without You *(lyrics)*

I gave you all my adoration,
I carried a torch for you,
I thought you were my only inspiration,
the only thing in my life that was true,

But now I see
That everything I loved in you is also in me,
And now I know
The power and the beauty of my own light,
So I'm letting it show,
And I can do this and I will do this, even without you.
Yes, I can do this and I will do this, even without you.

For locked up in the seed is a beautiful tree,
But within that hardened shell it can never be free,
Until our tears dissolve the seed coat,
which in an instant splits apart...
And that's what is meant by `the breaking of the heart'...

When you left me I just felt I'd died, dear,
from emptiness deep within,
I thought I couldn't bear the pain inside, dear,
I didn't know where I could even begin.

But now I see
The side-effect of losing you is discovering me,
And now I know
That miracles can manifest through me,
So I'm letting them grow,
And I can do this and I will do this, even without you.
Yes, I can do this and I will do this, even without you...

The Flame (lyrics)

When the pain becomes too much for me to bear,
When I cry aloud for help, but no-one's there,
When the path is long and steep,
and there's no-one as my guide,
I become the Flame; I light the Flame inside!

I am not this body, I am not this pain,
I am not extinguished by endless storms and rain,
You can hate me or despise me,
but you can't put out my light,
I am the Flame: I'll keep on burning bright!

I am not the mourner paralysed by loss,
I am not the ego that longs to be the boss,
I am not that hollow loneliness that yearns for someone's kiss,
I am the Flame: I'm so much more than this!

I am not the stories that I used to tell,
Problems, drama, trauma, and feeling so unwell,
I am not the helpless victim who does nothing but endure,
I am the Flame: I'm truly so much more!

When the pain becomes too much for us to bear,
When we cry aloud for help, but no-one's there,
When the path is long and steep,
and there's no-one as our guide,
We become the Flame; we light the Flame inside!

Let your heart remember what it's always known,
Feel the fire within you, and know you're not alone,
We will forge a new community, ignite the healing ways,
We are the Flame: let's set the world ablaze!

ACCEPTANCE

Sacred time is a circle

Sacred time is a circle, not a line. Our life revolves
around a centre, though we may not know it. In the seasons
there is rhythm.

If clocks are circles, it is calendars that make the myth
that time goes by, and things are passed by time.
Development, they call it.
We run as if on treadmills, trying to catch up
with something that has gone, or run into a future
that we do not know.

Sacred time is the wheel of the year, and within it
the cycles of the moon: new moon, waxing, half to full,
then half and waning, once again to new.
The solstice and the equinox,
the festivals between them,
all marked out around the circle,
as we hold space for each other,
and share, and sing.

GRATITUDE

Limitless Flow (lyrics)

All that we focus on
just keeps on coming back again:
Money or poverty,
love or anger, joy or pain.
With so much I cannot change,
I choose to change my attitude,
Calling in the life I want
with this song of gratitude:

I am grateful for the limitless flow
of abundance in my life!

Grateful for morning sun
and colours of the evening skies,
Songbirds and flowering trees,
cats and dogs and butterflies.
Grateful for the air I breathe,
for water and the food I eat,
Grateful for my head and heart,
grateful for my hands and feet.

I am grateful for the limitless flow
of abundance in my life!

Money is sacred
energy made tangible,
It flows in and flows out,
its powers are incredible:
Feeding me and clothing me,
taking me to somewhere new,
Leading me to people that
I can feel connected to.

I am grateful for the limitless flow
of abundance in my life!

Troubles have come and gone,
I've always made it through somehow:
See me still standing here:
wiser, braver, stronger now,
Grateful for these challenges,
I know that they're remaking me,
Giving me the strength to go
wherever life is taking me.

I am grateful for the limitless flow
of abundance in my life!

Grateful for people who
bring me gifts and help me out,
Good friends and family,
that's what life is all about:

Grateful for the seeds of love
that start to sprout and grow in me,
Grateful for the streams of love
that bubble up and flow in me.

I am grateful for the limitless flow
of abundance in my life!

Celebrating GREEN WEEK

GREEN! is reviving me
making the blood sparkle in my veins again
after the prickly pain of parched yellow grass
and the unyielding hardness of cold grey stone
convinced me that something vital in me had died

GREEN! like the healing song
that the ancestors sang millennia before
in the sacred groves and the mountain shrines
as they drank of the herbs that held within them
atoms from their own forefathers' breath

(sometimes the sun) but this too shall pass
(sometimes the rain) but this too shall pass

and some rejoice in the sun and curse the rain
and others rejoice in the rain and curse the sun

but the reality is that you and I and all that is **GREEN!**
would not be able to exist
unless there was an exquisite
balance between the two

(sometimes joy) but this too shall pass
(sometimes grief) but this too shall pass

so I bring my tears here and they become the rain
so I bring my scorching love and it becomes the sun
and I see how the rock is covered by soft moss
and I see how the new grass grows tender and fresh

GREEN! is showing me
a way of gratitude
and I can be thankful for both love and loss

COURAGE

While We're Here (lyrics)

I wonder what you might attempt,
if you knew you could not fail...
Where would you go, what would you do,
if you were not afraid?
What would you dream, what would you try?
Where would you climb, how far, how high?
Where would you go, what would you do,
if you were not afraid?

Where would you sing, how would you dance,
if you knew no-one would judge you?
Where would you go, what would you do,
if you could break through fear?
What long-kept secret would you share?
What would you give to show you care?
Where would you go, what would you do,
if you could break through fear?

When will we take that leap of faith?
We've waited long enough!
When will we understand
that we are more than strong enough?
When will we hear that inner voice that waits to guide us,
To light the flame of love that burns so deep inside us?
When will we let determination cast out fear?
When will we realise, when will we realise,
We've got to live each moment while we're here?

What are the words that you would say,
if you could not be rejected?
Where would you go, what would you do,
with a courageous heart?
What grievance would you rise above?
To whom would you declare your love?
Where would you go, what would you do,
with a courageous heart?

When will we take that leap of faith?
We've waited long enough!...
When will we understand
that we are more than strong enough?
When will we hear that inner voice that waits to guide us,
To light the flame of love that burns so deep inside us?
When will we let determination cast out fear?
When will we realise, when will we realise,
We've got to live each moment while we're here?

The songs of those who leave us
often have a common chorus,
Regretting not the things they've done,
but what they didn't do:
The paths not taken, chances missed,
The people that they never kissed...
Where can we go, what can we do,
although we're still afraid?

Today we take that leap of faith! We've waited long enough...
Today we understand that we are more than strong enough!
Let's listen to that inner voice that waits to guide us,
To light the flame of love that burns so deep inside us:
Today we let determination cast out fear;
Today we realise, today we realise,
We've got to live each moment while we're here!

One Small Step (lyrics)

I'm taking this one small step beyond the world I know,
Today I will reach a place I've never dared to go,
And I just don't care what people say,
I'm gonna feel the fear and do it anyway:
I'm taking that one small step that lets my passion grow...

Because life was meant for living, for exploring and forgiving,
Doesn't matter if they call me mad or weird or strange:
For I may never get another chance
to join this wild and crazy dance,
I can't keep waiting around for someone else to change!

I'm taking this one small step that brings my soul alive,
With barriers breaking down, my heart's in overdrive,
Don't you tell me that it can't be done,
'Cause I will not give up before I have begun:
I'm taking that one small step, just watch me learn to thrive!

I'm taking this one small step: oh, can you understand?
On days when I don't feel brave,
will you please hold my hand?
Will you show me that I'm not alone,
And will you find a step that you can call your own?
For when we step up together, we can change this land!

Because life was meant for living, for exploring and forgiving,
Doesn't matter if they call us mad or weird or strange:
For we may never get another chance
to join this wild and crazy dance,
We can't keep waiting around for someone else to change!

EXCITEMENT

Now's The Time (lyrics)

Now's the time, and I'm ready for the next step,
Now's the time, and I'm ready to shine,
Now's the time, and I'm ready to speak out louder,
And claim the life that was always meant to be mine!

I've got a dream in my soul, and I'll chase it,
And I have faith it'll chase me, in turn;
I feel the fear, but I'm learning to face it,
For I will not be the candle that keeps refusing to burn!

I've got a plan, I can't wait to begin it,
I've got a stage and a role I can play;
I know the game, and I know I can win it,
Now I can finally say what I've always wanted to say...

I feel awakened, empowered, inspired,
I feel the flow and it's setting me free;
I've got the courage to do what's required,
For I am figuring out what it really means to be me!

PRIDE

Coming Out Of My Chrysalis (lyrics)

I'm coming out of my chrysalis now,
I want to break out and touch the limitless sky,
So I am finding my courage somehow,
For I've been growing these wings,
And I think I might be ready to fly;
I'm coming out of my chrysalis now!

Here in the dark I've been transforming,
growing my rainbow wings,
Now, with the sunlight's gentle warming,
see what the new day brings:
This is my moment, I'm deciding,
this is my time to go;
All of the talents I've been hiding,
I'm gonna put on show...
I'm coming out of my chrysalis now!

But I never thought that it would take this long,
And I just don't know if I can be that strong;
Who'd have ever thought
that coming out could hurt this way?

So if it's not too late,
I think I'll change my mind and stay...

No, I can't be me when I am stuck in here!
Got to find a way through all this doubt and fear,
Because from far away I hear the flowers calling me...
And now I realise how much they need me to be free!

Flowers, I hear you, just stay strong now,
I will be with you soon;
Light's breaking through, it won't be long now,
tearing this thin cocoon,
I wasn't made to crawl forever, nettles are not my world,
One final push, it's now or never...
See me with wings unfurled!

See, I've come out of that chrysalis now,
I've broken out now to greet the limitless sky;
For I discovered my courage somehow,
Just see these beautiful wings,
Now I know at last I'm ready to fly!
Who needs that empty old chrysalis now?

Your 'AFAB' Does Not Erase Me

Yes, I was assigned-female-at-birth,
grew up behind net curtains with my secrets concealed inside,
where nobody (and least of all me)
understood quite what was denied.
I refused to answer to my given name at five,
hid growing curves under baggy sweaters at twelve,
felt weird and wrong
around girls who wore make-up and heels
and spent their weekends shopping for pink lace bras:
that was all I knew. There were things that I never tried to do,
because it just wasn't 'done', within that net; and many things
that I didn't say, and couldn't have said, however I tried,
because the words weren't even invented yet.
There wasn't a language, then, for people like me.
#TransgenderBoy and #TransgenderMan were years away,
The teachers could have been fired just for saying 'gay'.
So, in conclusion: secrets: kept.

Yet your 'AFAB' cannot define me now.
#WontBeErased #WontBeDenied
My #ExistenceIsResistance;
and if you dare try to delete me, I WILL resist.
Assigning pink lace flowers to hide what you can't accept
can no more erase the blue core of a #TransGuy like me
than King Canute's command 'Thus far, and no further'
could ever hold back the inrushing Solent tide. Whatever
you choose to call me, whatever you say, I will ride the waves
to places you never dreamed, and live my self-made life
as my truest self anyway.

There's no way in again, now I'm out.
Because this is who I am, and have always been,
and the only alternative is...

                          No.
                          Let's not go there.

I am here.
Defiantly turquoise.
Dynamic.
Impassioned.
Alive.

So take your eraser, take your net curtains, and go;
I am still here, no longer silent, at this meeting-place
of sea and shore, persistently pushing on as the waves do,
and reminding myself day after day that there are more
ways than one to be a man. There are more ways than one
for the deep essence of a human soul to survive.

EUPHORIA

Who We Are (lyrics)

There's no dream too big for us,
and in our souls we always knew it:
We've waved goodbye to doubts and fears,
and now we're certain we can do it...
We've seen the way that things can be,
now it's our time, the world is waiting...
With shining eyes we spread the word
about the vision we're creating.

Now the spark at the centre of the spiral is alight,
and we're on fire,
And the energy of love flows through us,
bringing all that we desire...
See us spinning in space like a cosmic superstar,
Now we've woken up and remembered who we are.

Touch a heart, transform a life:
for us it only takes a minute.
And if we don't know where we're going,
let's just trust, and then begin it...

Let's make some miracles today,
we are the source of hope and healing:
We'll sing it all from soul to soul,
there is no language for this feeling!

Now the spark at the centre of the spiral is alight,
and we're on fire,
And the energy of love flows through us,
bringing all that we desire...
See us spinning in space like a cosmic superstar,
Now we've woken up and remembered who we are.

Who you are is who I am,
and who we are is the beginning,
We are the light, we are the love
that keeps the stars and planets spinning:
We stand united and we know
the time has come to reconnect now,
And we'll create a way of living
built on justice and respect now!

When the spark at the centre of the spiral's set alight,
you'll be on fire,
Let the energy of love flow through you,
bringing all that you desire...
Join us spinning in space like a cosmic superstar,
Now you've woken up and remembered who you are.

Rainbow Fuzziness
(Inspired by an artwork by Aliya Cambray)

Showing my true colours now,
dancing, swaying in bright stripes,
putting myself in your hands:
will you hold me? Can you see
the euphoria that lights me up inside
when I find myself here, safe, loved,
in this soft rainbow fuzziness that's so much more
than pride?

FEAR

Trans Night of Too Much Visibility
(Written in response to an artwork by Debbie Goatley Birch)

Overvisible in the glare
of the station lights at night. Too bright. They stare
at the facial hair you didn't have time to shave,
and my curves that won't lie flat anymore since the cough
forced me to take the binder off.
We've got this.
Breathe.
They stare. So what?

Five of them and two of us, that's what.
Quicken your pace. Just a bit.
Ssssh. Don't speak out loud. They'll know.
Look relaxed. Fake it. We'll make it. *Shit.*
It'll be fine. Don't fuss.
Are they laughing at me? At you?
At both of us?

Take me out of this place, this space,
this placespacetrace of overcolour overnoise
overwhelm... and back to the place
where I can be
just be
be free
be
me

FRUSTRATION

The Oracle Has Spoken
(Inspired by the artwork 'The Oracle of Gender Determination' by Jani E. Z. Franck)

The Oracle has spoken. This part
of the flesh defines it all; so be thou classified!
The choice is made for us. All must be organised,
analysed, overdictated. Simplified. Objectified.
Recombobulated.
We are minutes old. Minutes.
At this age, how do you know?
How do you know what you think you know?
Your verdict misgenders futures. Where do we go,
when the walls collapse to the size of a box on a page?
M or F. F or M. She/her/he/him.... they? Them?
What if there isn't a box or a word?
Will we remain forever mis-seen, mis-known, misheard?
So tell me again (maybe you said it and I missed it)...
What *did* the oracle say? And is today the day
when you might, perhaps, be ready
to resist it?

DEFIANCE

Rebel Warriors

Caught up in the shadow-plays
on the paper-thin screen,
the dramas staged to distract us
from where we are and who we could be:

some characters fight over sovereignty,
some squabble for oil and dollars,
some mourn for the lost days of empire;
while the seas fill with plastic
and the skies start to suffocate us
and forests burn, rivers flood, rains fail,
and poison nectar paralyses bees' tongues
and the flowers die unpollinated
and the last turtle,
unnoticed,
breathes her last breath.

They call us hypocrites
when we sit down on the bridge.

They complain that we use mobile phones,
drink bottled water,
eat industrial food,
wear clothes made with child labour,
ride on fossil-fuelled buses and trains
instead of walking a hundred miles.

Then they mock the few who come on foot,
wearing their homespun clothes,
eating their home-grown salads,
as overprivileged white
middle-class festival-goers.

The truth is,
they have no truth to throw at us,
and they know it, when we steal
a glimpse through the torn tissue of lies
and see our future in flames.

They will carry us away one by one,
they will dismantle our barricades,
but nothing will be the same again.

We have started to feel
the undeniable memory of earth energy
tingling in the soles of our bare feet.
We remember, with each insistent drumbeat,
the lifetimes when we gathered
to tell stories of the old heroes
and sing love-songs to the full moon.

We may yet fail. There may be no-one left
to look back with gratitude on this bridge
and tell the stories of us. But the moon,
silent then as now, will shine on the places
where our bones are buried; and wherever
or whatever we are by then, we will sing
the shining back to her, with the same love.

And she will know,
and we will know,
we tried.

Sigil
(Inspired by the artwork 'Truth Sigil' by Jani E. Z. Franck)

With the power of Air and Sacred Sky,
With the powers of Fire and Water and Earth
I charge you; fly
With the power of Deep Mystery,
the Love beyond all names,
Reveal the hidden Truth
transcending petty power games.

Reveal the hidden motives and reveal the lies,
Reveal the loveless hearts
of those who claim to represent us, but despise
all that we are and all we stand for
(even as they pledge to save
our lives with those same policies that drove us,
almost, to the grave).

Pierce through the bluster like an arrow
so we see, with open eyes,
the emptiness of promises and mantras
they have chanted for so long –
reused, revived, rehashed – and ultimately
let ourselves concede
that they were wrong.
`Get Brexit done.' Is Brexit truly what we need,
or is the deep desire of every heart to find
those leaders who will dare
to stand against the rising tide of soul-despair
and speak of hope,
and after speaking, act, and act again,
until they prove they genuinely care?

Pierce through the apathy,
the disillusionment, the fear.
Remind the desperate that they have a choice;
the choice has never been so clear.
No-one is perfect, we are human,
but humility and love can conquer hate,
Truth may yet conquer lies; a block of melting ice
contributes more to the debate
than all the words that they refused to speak.
It's not too late to use our voice.

Fly then, sigil, with the powers of the elements;
help us all to understand.
May the Truth be seen
in all the four corners of the land!

EXASPERATION

Modern Fairy Tale

Once upon a time there was a trans man
who had two daughters.

You can't say 'Once upon a time there was a trans man'...

Why not?

There are no trans people in fairy stories.
Children aren't allowed
to know about trans people.

Why?
Because they're too frightening?
Don't give me that.
Fairy tales are full of monsters,
dragons, evil witches,
wicked sorcerers,
ogres and ugly-ass beasts,
and you're worried
that the children are going to be scared
by one little trans man?

It just doesn't work that way.
You'll have to make him
either a beast or a monster.

But he wasn't a beast or a monster.
He wasn't an ogre
or a dragon pretending to be human
or an evil sorcerer
or a cross-dressing witch.

He might have messed up a lot,
as we all do, but he meant well.
He was just a regular trans guy,
if slightly on the short side.

Ah, he was short!
That solves the problem.
Call him a hobbit,
and get on with the story.

OK, fine, if it makes you happy!
Although I really don't see...
But whatever.

    Once upon a time
    there was a transgender hobbit
    who had two daughters...

EMOTIONAL ROLLER-COASTER

A Lover's Guide to the Electromagnetic Spectrum

X. It starts with high energy: the invisible, the mystery,
uncharted territory, handled with caution, because
the unknown feels dangerous. Words penetrate to bone:
did I go too far? Will she take that wrong? Sign off: Xxx.

Ultraviolet. In the right light, a radiance: a glimmer of
something beyond ordinary. Shades shifted,
the commonplace becomes unearthly, the unseen
essence revealed. Heart-glow. Attraction undeniable.

Visible spectrum. Dressed in rainbows, dancing with pride,
daring the world to deny the brightness of our love.
Radiant in our true colours, complementing each other,
embracing without shame within a sea of queer kin.

Infrared. The warm glow of an autumn log fire,
murmur of conversation, drinks sipped. Hostile stares
from old white men who debate our existence: we dim
our light, invisible now to all on other wavelengths.

Microwave. No spoons left for cooking. Energy decreasing,
sapped by the deadening weight of creditors' letters
and casual misgendering and stressful jobs and online trolls.
Value lasagne is all we can afford. Two minutes. Done.

Radio. Classic FM plays on in the background as she tells me
there's someone else. They're in love. Waves lengthen to fade.
The music ends, the air ceases to vibrate. Words, unsaid,
hang in the space between us. The death of stars. Silence.

Author's Note: The next poem has a trigger warning for de-
pression and includes references to suicidal thoughts and self-
harm, although it ends on a more upbeat note with a survival
strategy.

TRIGGER WARNING:
DEPRESSION

Surviving (But Only Just)

My mind lies:
its fictions pound me with the force of vindictive ocean,
drowning out my soul-songs
in the clash of salt water on pebble shore.
Surges of inescapable emotion
taunt me with could-have-done-this
and would-have-done-that and should-have-known
and what-the-fuck-is-the-point-of-it-all and
who-am-I-even-doing-this-for-if I-just-end-up-alone and I
DON'T WANT TO BE HERE ANYMORE and I
Am. Just. So. Done. With. This. Life.
But I keep on typing,
because while my fingers are touching these keys
they're not holding the knife.

Every wave of words makes less sense than the last.
If anyone finds this after I'm gone,
they'll never get a grasp of the reasons why.
They'll say, *There WAS no reason for him to die:*
he must have been murdered by his own mind.

I did try.
I tried to tell the story of what brought me here,
to leave some meaningful explanation behind,
but it's turned to a perfect storm
of expletives and self-denigration,
paragraph breaks forgotten,
barely even a pause for punctuation. The hurricane builds,
scattering spellings too in its wake,
splitting my heart wide open
and spilling its distress on to the screen.

And yet I can't allow myself
to admit defeat, and abandon these keys for the knife,
and leave a gory mess
for some poor soul to find. If only this rupture of the heart
could be more than a metaphor; but a haemorrhage of words
can never suffice to silence this despised beat.

At last, after three thousand words,
the storm subsides.

I pause.
Breathe.
Survey the detritus.
Ctrl-A.
Delete.

The sea, gentle now at low tide, murmurs to me the names
of friends who might hold my voice to their ear,
like a shell whispering ancient songs,

and remind me how to remind myself
that this, too, shall pass; and I am not, in fact, alone.
The sliver of glass impaling my heart
has turned to sea-glass, jagged points worn smooth,
summoning just enough courage
to reach for the phone and send a text:

How are you doing? Sorry I haven't called. Sorry I couldn't
make it last Friday. It's been a rough few days.
Not doing great.
Not in the best place.

Surely someone must hear what lies behind
these bland understatements that are all I have in me now,
and understand the unspoken cry? *I'm surviving, but only just.*
I still want to die. But I don't.
I need you, badly. Help me find
a way to stop believing the lies told by my mind...

ANGUISH

Make More Bad Art, They Said

Ouch! Fuck this. Painting hurts.
Why is this painting breaking my heart? Is it the stroke
of colour whose beauty is lost
in an instant, that leaves me bleeding from the soul;
or is it the beauty beyond the brushstroke's reach,
never-quite-visible, never-quite-knowable,
that scrapes away at the hollow place inside?

Stop asking why. It doesn't matter *why*.
At least you're feeling something! Even if it hurts.
Wouldn't it be nice if, just once, you could stay
with the pain, could let it be what it is,
instead of overthinking it until you're numb?
In the end, it isn't what you make of the canvas
that matters; it's what the canvas
makes of *you*. Canvas can be given away,
ripped into shreds, sacrificed to the elements:
'Air' hung from a tree to be battered by gales,
'Fire' burned to ashes, 'Water' left out in the rain,
'Earth' buried as food for the fungoid realms.

Or sold, if you can find the right formula: sold,
if the equation between fame, scarcity and desire
flips in your favour, for a lifetime's salary,
ten lifetimes, more. (Though probably not.)

None of that matters.
The brush, every time it glides across the canvas
to deposit a layer of paint, removes a layer
of rust from the heart. One layer closer
to the authenticity of you.
That's why it fucking hurts. There's nowhere to hide.

Keep making that godawful mess. Keep splodging
that disgusting neon yellow in with the green.
Keep screwing it up. Again and again and – *fuck* – again.

Oh God, I had it for a second.
I had it. That streak of colour.
The one streak of colour
that said it all. It was THERE
but I didn't know when to stop
(I never know when to stop)
and then I screwed it up
(the way I always do)
and it was gone.

It doesn't matter that it's gone.
You had it for a second.
It had *you* for a second.
It'll have you again.
Keep going. Make more bad art.
Bad art will be the making of you.

RAGE

The Tarantella of the Plague-Spirits

Do you remember the death-fires burning?
Do you remember the flame,
And the choking smoke and the fears it awoke,
And the light that dies in an orphan's eyes,
And the charred remains of fur?
And the fields you ploughed and the loud angry crowd,
And the innocents staring in silent yearning;
Do you remember the death-fires burning?
Do you remember the flame?
And the fields that you ploughed, and the loud angry crowd,
Calling curses from the land that you couldn't understand,
And the venom and the rage and the blame?
And the dying screams
Of the dreams
Of the mothers who blessed and caressed
Every child that they bore?
Are you sure
you'll endure
all the fallout from the war
that you waged on the forest with your flame?
Do you feel any shame?

Will you confess your guilt in words,
Or are you choked with soot?

Never forget the burning.
Never forget.
Know that we haunt you yet.
We have followed you, unseen, with no regrets,
In the death-bringing breath
Of the trauma survivors you trafficked away
To be butchered for meat or sold as pets.
Will the money that you made from blood and oil
And the dust that once was fertile soil
Help you at all when we wither your tongues,
And set the death-fires alight in your lungs?
Will you know the worth
Of the forests that were called the lungs of the Earth,
When we hang their loss
Round your necks like an albatross?

GRIEF

How am I? (COVID-19 Lockdown, Day 4)

How am I? Am I OK?
I don't know what that means any more.
I know that I've been crying more tears in the past six days
than in the six weeks that went before. But I can breathe,
and I'm grateful for that. I'm working,
or keeping up some pretence of trying.
Nothing makes sense; but it makes no less
sense to me than anyone else, I guess. I'm breaking down,
or breaking open, I don't know. But, at least, not dying.

Peeling my life back to the bare bones. Going within,
and going without. Trying to work out if there's
some deeper purpose behind it all, some bigger Reason Why.
Bypassing. Keeping my vibe high.
Then not bypassing, because bypassing doesn't cut it.
Diving head-first into the vile mess.
Disintegrating? Healing?
Making friends with the distress I'm feeling?

No idea.

Revealing layers of grief
that I didn't know were there.
Trying to care. Trying not to care.
Who cares? Who knows?
No different, in that respect,
from anyone else, I suppose.

But I'm safe, as far as I can tell.
So I guess I should probably say
I'm doing well.

How about you?

AMUSEMENT

Online Choir (to the tune of 'Do You Hear The People Sing?')

Can you hear the people sing?
Not at the moment, they're on mute!
Yes, I can see their mouths are moving
And they're looking kind of cute,
But I only hear myself,
What kind of singalong is that?
Tell me, how will I even know if I'm going flat?

When we gathered for our singsongs,
We'd have soup and home-made bread,
Now I'm singing to a screen and drinking
Cup-a-Soup instead!
But what can I say?
Well, it's better than ending up dead...

We look forward to our Zoom calls,
and they help us all stay strong,
Make our Sunday evenings brighter,
and the weeks not quite so long...
Our friendship's unchanging,
No virus can silence our song!

BOREDOM

Disco 2020 (lyrics)
To the tune of 'Disco 2000' by Pulp

It's seven weeks since I set eyes on my mother,
And even longer since you last saw your brother,
You've shaved your hair off now
(It never suited you...)
Did you dream that when we grew up
We'd go for months and never meet up?
No, I didn't either,
Never even thought of it...

So are you climbing the wall?
Does the house feel much too small?
If I came round to call,
No further than your hall,
Well, would you let me in at all?'

And they all said,
`Let's all meet up in cyberspace now!
Won't it be fun when we all dance on Zoom?
Be there two o'clock in the safety of your room...

I know you're home, there's no excuses,
I know you've been living down there on your own,
Since that damp and lonely Thursday months ago...
What are you doing Sunday, baby?
Do you fancy online yoga, maybe?
Hey, hey, please unmute me, baby...'
Woo woo woo woo woo woo woo...

I was the first in my street to go out
The neighbours said, 'What's that all about?'
Oh, I thought I'd love it but I was a mess:
Too many humans, and it caused me such stress!
To the shop, that was as far as I went
I could have exercised sometimes but it meant...
Oh, it meant nothing to me
Cause I'm such a lazy bum...

So are you climbing the wall?
Does your life feel much too small,
If I came round to call,
No further than your hall,
Well, would I get a hug at all?

And they all said,
'Welcome to Disco 2020,
Hugging is history, let's just dance on Zoom!
It's better to stay in the safety of your room:
Pour your own drink and let's get pissed now,
Puke in the sink and clean up on your own,
Cause your cleaner's not allowed in, don't you know?

What are you doing Sunday, baby?
Oops, it's blurring into Monday, maybe,
What the actual fuck, it's Thursday, baby?!
Woo woo woo woo woo woo woo,
Woo woo woo woo woo...

ANXIETY

Covidless People (lyrics)
To the tune of 'Common People' by Pulp

I want to live like Covidless people,
I want to do what Covidless people do,
Want to stay safe like Covidless people,
Want to stay safe like Covidless people like you,
So what else should I do?

I'm going to the supermarket
No delivery slots, I need some food from somewhere
So I'll get it there
Queue outside for half an hour
Got no bloody eggs or flour but it's fine
At least they've got loo roll this time!

They've painted arrows on the floor now
It's meant to help you feel secure now
(Doesn't work)
I try to keep two metres' distance
My efforts meet with much resistance
On the part of the guy who's going the wrong damn way
(What a jerk)

He just doesn't understand
And he didn't even sanitise his hands

Stand behind the second line
Put your mask on, you'll be fine
No-one cares if you can breathe
As long as you don't cough or sneeze
Forget the cash, just use your card
Look, it's really not that hard
You can speak but just step back
If you get too close, someone might attack, so...

Play along with the Covidless people
Play along and it might just get you through
Play along with the Covidless people
Play along and pray it stays away from you
Because there's nothing else to do...

Binder
I put my binder on
for the first time in twelve days
and within an hour
developed a cough.
I told myself
it was psychosomatic.
All in my mind, I said.
I'm *fine*, I said.
But, all the same,
just in case,
I still took it off.

Author's Note: The poems in the 'Despair' chapter (*Sometimes Waving but Mostly Drowning* and *Free Speech*) have a trigger warning for suicidal thoughts, transphobic and homophobic hate crimes, physical assault, emotional abuse of children, and cyberbullying. To skip ahead to something more uplifting, go to the `Perseverance' chapter for a poem written specifically for survivors of hate crime.

TRIGGER WARNING: DESPAIR

Sometimes Waving but Mostly Drowning

"I was much too far out all my life /
And not waving but drowning" – Stevie Smith

Page after page, the shit rolls in:
hysterical headlines that seem so real
to those beyond our circle, inked in lies,
telling the middle-class bigots
that we're the target group they're still permitted to despise.
Page after page.
Wave after wave of mindless rage.
As if our eyes can't see, our hearts can't feel.

Thugs on the streets or the buses,
throwing rocks or punches at us for holding hands.
Mumsnet mums on their phones throwing digital slurs,
as they pack their children's lunches
in eco-friendly paper bags and tie
pink bands around their perfect plaits:

all of them running so damn scared
because we, the gender rebels, dared
to cut our hair and wear
a shirt and tie, and live as the men we are;
or grow our hair and wear
a skirt and tights, and live as the women that we are;
or dye our hair multiple shades of blue and wear
rainbow unicorn socks
and refuse to tick ANY fucking gender box
(or indeed any combination of the above that might suggest
for a millisecond that we love and accept ourselves the way
we truly are)... none of it matters, in the end,
because the only way to play
the game is their way, they say:
to shine the masks up and pretend.
Conform, they tell us; heaven knows we tried, we *tried*,
we thought we could forget the truth of who we always were,
and just play small, and hide...
until the weight of masks began to suffocate us,
and the exhaustion of pretence began to break us
somewhere deep inside...
until the moment came to realise it was *this or die*...
    and some chose this,
    and others died.

Our non-compliance is a threat, or so it seems,
to the existence of their dreams
of 'Man-The-Head'; to the extent
that in the eyes, still blurred with lies,
of those who think they know it all,
we would be better dead.

Our flag is life and hope, within our circle; but to them
offensive, painting the sky with
words they wish they never had to hear.
And still, wave after wave, the shit rolls nearer.
Photographs of those they hurt. Nazis escorted by police,
to keep them safe while they attack our Pride.
(And what about OUR safety? Don't we count?)
Swastikas flying freely, flouting law,
and our flag trampled in the dirt and blood and mud...
and we, thrown here and there by every wave,
half-broken, all exhausted,
wash up now in some dark cave,
as with our final strength
we gather up the remnants of our flag
from seaweed-slimy rocks,
and wash the stink of fascists from our skin;

and yet again,
the mothers, frowning
as we proclaim our right to breathe,
begin a new petition.

And we are here,
still here,
still calling out for allies
to join our coalition of the brave,
sometimes waving...
but, if I'm honest,
mostly drowning.

Free Speech

Sticks and stones can break bones;
they don't hurt like a song can,
For something that sticks in your head for so long can
Still haunt you for years when the scars have all faded,
And taunt you on nights when you're tired and jaded.
Those bones would have healed in a month, maybe two,
But that's nothing compared to what singing can do!
(Some scientists proved it. Old songs still leave traces
In brains that forget their own grandchildren's faces.)
Whoever said words didn't matter was lying:
They can't be unheard, and there's no point in trying,
For decades of therapy fly out the door
When there's nothing else left in my brain any more
But the song the boys sang on the sixteenth of May, '84.

OK, I admit it. I made up the date, and
it might have been March
that those kids sung their hate, and
I said '84 because that was the year that
some George dude predicted repression and fear that
would shut people's mouths, which is kind of ironic,
'cause now songs go viral and hate's electronic.
I'll get to that later. The point is, it's shocking
That four decades on from the taunting and mocking,
My brain has wiped out all the faces and names
(Though I know it was started by Matthew or James)
But at three in the morning the words that I hear
Are that same fucking song coming through loud and clear
And that voice won't shut up and I wish I could just disappear.

Sticks and stones can break bones;
they don't hurt you like words do.
I used to think tweeting was something that birds do:
But now every writer who's left feeling bitter
Can pour out their hatred on something called Twitter
And claim they've been muted. Can *you* hear their silence?
Their words on a screen are incitement to violence,
They say they've been cancelled, with platforms no less
Than ten million strong in the popular press,
And they make a loud noise and cry, 'Speech must be free!'
As they voice their opinions on who I can be
But they're free to proclaim that I shouldn't be free to be me.

They call for 'fair play' – well, who doesn't love fairness?
They say all they're doing is 'raising awareness'
Or 'safeguarding children, defending their rights'.
They would strongly deny that they're here to start fights
As they tell politicians that getting their 'X'
Is conditional, now, on respecting their sex.
What d'you mean, who's their ex? I don't know and don't care.
I'm not that kind of poet. Look, let's not go there.
They can have all the sex that they want, and that's fine.
They can live their own lives and just let me live mine!
But it's my fault, of course, if I dare to be loud
And be true to myself, and come out, and be proud:
For their darling great-niece has become a 'trans-trender'
All thanks to yours truly expressing his gender.
They can't use the changing rooms, much less the loo,
Because trans women use them. (So what if they do?
Their junk makes them dysphoric,
so why would they show it to *you*?)

We're completely to blame, so they say, for the rain,
And the COVID pandemic, and war in Ukraine,
And the trans women winning gold medals – wait, what?
Which women, which medals?? Perhaps I forgot...
And it's our fault 'the whole fucking world has turned woke',
And it's our fault they're lonely, and our fault they're broke,
And it's our fault – what now? Is there something I've missed?
Yes, we've threatened the freedom on which they insist!
But they're still free to say that we shouldn't be free
to exist.

OVERWHELM

Moving House, With Dyspraxia

when your thoughts (which were already scattered)
are now half-in and half-out of fourteen
(coffee!) half-made cardboard boxes
and the (what time
is the cleaner coming?
fuck, that clashes with a Zoom call...)
and *coffee!*

and work just
keeps on piling up
in the corner
with the sweepings from
the kitchen floor
(where the fuck did the dustpan go?)

and you're still wondering
when you'll get to that thing which was due
two weeks ago and (oh shit that other whatsname which was
due three and a half weeks ago) and (ugh missed the
deadline for submitting that whatdjamacallit)

and you can't remember if the carpet guy got back to you
and you think you might have accidentally booked
two cleaners and no painter
and you haven't even given a thought to the
electrician, and (argh, there's a stain on the curtain too)
and that melted patch of carpet haunts your dreams
(and Facebook breaks your heart
four times before breakfast) and COFFEE!!!

and you've got 33 minutes
before the first Zoom of the day

and those boxes
are still looking at you
along with the landlady's 6-page checking-out checklist
and you can't remember
which box you put your sanity in
(if you ever had any in the first place)
and you still haven't found the dustpan
and (grind the beans)

and... ooh, this is a super interesting article!
(but you realise your lifelong dream is now impossible
because by the time you retire
Anglesey will be underwater)

and fuck the policing and crime bill
and fuuuuuuck racists
and (turn the machine on and oh fuck it all
you forgot to put the ground coffee in again
and now you have a cup of water)

and empty it out and start again and this time possibly
remember to heat up the milk and
(what do you mean you're
exhausted just reading it?) and yeah instant coffee
is a thing but it doesn't taste like the *real* thing

and images from dreams keep intruding
and *I'm trying to save a random person*
from choking to death on their own vomit
after taking too many drugs and
(yeah, that part was a dream
but everything else in this pocm is true
and not even exaggerated)

and ugh
boxes everywhere

and (got to pick up that airbed pump) and your friend's
coming tomorrow to cut the hedge but only if it doesn't rain,
and if it rains you'll have to postpone
and (shit, never sent those photos (or that email))
and now we're on to double brackets
(how did it even take this long?)
(COFFEEE!!!)
and (somebody help me here I'm drowning) and (argh,
now I've switched pronouns (am I an I or are you a you?))
and I've lost track of the brackets)) (I can't track it,
the bracket) (fuck dyspraxia fuck it all)
(s o m e b o d y h e l p m e)
(**COFFEEEEEEEE....**)

and the coffee machine overflows
and then you cut your knee
on the broken broom.

Mop up the blood.
Put on the work face.
Click 'Join Call'.
Aaaaaand..... smile.

The move?
Yeah, it's going well, thanks.

PERSEVERANCE

Hang On In There
(An open letter to survivors of hate crime)

So somebody hates you, and everything's dark?
Ignore them. Keep living. The world needs your spark.
There's plenty of haters: sure, that much is clear,
But the thing that annoys them is seeing us here,
So don't check out now, please. Stay here. Don't give in.
Let's keep on annoying them. Don't let them win.

They took out their anger and sadness on you:
We see how it's hurt you, and we're hurting, too:
They've ripped us to shreds and they've ruined our days,
And we're stuck back together in very strange ways.
There's no way to go back and undo the harm,
But our crazy new shapes have... their own kind of charm.

The journey is long but you've travelled so far,
Fought so many fears to become who you are:
And yes, you're amazing! You'll say it's not true,
But there's someone out there who's inspired by you.
There's someone who sees you and loves what they see,
And thinks, 'Hey, one day maybe that will be me!'

It's OK to admit that you don't feel OK,
It's OK not to wash all the dishes today,
It's OK to sigh deeply and go back to bed
When you can't get away from the thoughts in your head;
But what isn't OK is to quit on us now:
Resolve to keep going, and soon you'll learn how.

The kids of the future will look back, bemused
At the way human beings were once so abused
For being themselves and for living their lives;
They'll admire the way that the spirit survives.
So come on. We've got this. The haters can't win.
Keep hanging on in there. Don't ever give in!

THE RETURN OF HOPE

Hymn to a River Goddess (lyrics)

Ancasta, rise for the ones who were forgotten,
Ancasta, rise for the ones who passed unmourned;
As the river, swift and free,
flows unhindered to the sea,
Let the pain of generations be transformed...

Let all who have awoken help us raise this timeless call:
Lady of the Waters, rise in us and change it all...
Wash away our pain and trauma,
wash away our doubts and fears,
Bring us back our ancient wisdom,
bring us back our stolen years!

Ancasta, rise for your healers and priestesses,
Ancasta, rise for the ones who called your name,
Cast your spell and wove your charm,
wished no ill and did no harm,
As with love and faith they lit your sacred flame...

Ancasta, rise for your artists and your dreamers,
Ancasta, rise for the ones who walked the Land,
For the ones who died too young,
for the songs that went unsung,
For the conquerors who could not understand...

Ancasta, rise now for those who shape the future,
Ancasta, rise for the healing of the Earth:
Let the love-songs that we sing
by the Itchen's hidden spring
Bring the hope of re-enchantment and rebirth!

Let all who have awoken help us raise this timeless call:
Lady of the Waters, rise in us and change it all...
Wash away our pain and trauma,
wash away our doubts and fears,
Bring us back our ancient wisdom,
bring us back our stolen years!

Author's Note: This poem was inspired by the band
Ancasta Rising, which in turn was inspired by a Roman
altar found in the River Itchen at the former settle-
ment of Clausentum, now the Bitterne Manor area in
my home town of Southampton. The stone artefact,
which is now in Sea City Museum, bears the inscrip-
tion *DEAE ANCASTAE GEMINVS MANI VSLM* - translated
as 'To the Goddess Ancasta, Geminus Mani[lius] will-
ingly and deservedly fulfills his vow.'.

Someday (lyrics)

You're never enough, you're always to blame,
You can't change your looks, your pronouns, your name,
Whatever you say, they still turn away;
you're forced to comply.
And so you grow up, just learning to hide:
You shut yourself down and keep it inside,
You're learning your part and doubting your heart,
believing the lie;

They say that you're broken, or evil, or wrong:
Don't listen! You know who you are. Just stay strong.
They tell you you're sinful, and offer to pray:
Don't listen! Don't listen!
You'll live as your true self, someday.

You put on the costumes, cover the scar,
Remember your lines, reject who you are:
You'll never explain the depth of this pain,
don't bother to try!
So as the years pass, you're less and less real,
You just give a shrug when asked how you feel,
And still, all the while, you're faking a smile,
and wanting to die...

They still say you're broken, or evil, or wrong...
Don't listen! You know who you are. Just stay strong.
They tell you you're sinful, and offer to pray:
Don't listen! Don't listen!
You'll live as your true self, someday.

So never give up and never give in,
Just trust in your heart and change can begin,
The truth that you see is setting you free,
you cannot deny;
We're here for you now, you're never alone,
You've travelled so far, and look how you've grown:
In finding your voice, you're making a choice
to reach for the sky!

It's not you that's broken, or evil, or wrong:
We're in this together, we've got this, stay strong!
Whatever they tell you, just say that you'll pray
That someday they'll listen,
they'll hear you, they'll see you, someday...

INSPIRATION

Breathe
(Written in response to an artwork by Orlando Myxx)

Pose, repose, re-pose, recline
in the mystery. In this moment
we are all divine. Lie back, relax.
Back in the time before the beginning,
when space held the possibilities of
any-and-every-not-yet-thing,
spinning in spirals. We breathe.

Sink into the leaves. All is well is all.
Stretch out and unfurl. *Breathe.* Uncurl
from the tight knots of tension.
Could we be real?
Be ourselves.
Be whole.
Be unafraid
to feel...

Open
(Written in response to an artwork by Jack Pudding)

And then the heart opens, and we gaze out from the cave
across the still expanse of not-yet-known
where yes, we have the permission to dwell
in darkness even while sunlight sparkles on the sea:
free not to go gently into the night,
to rage against the tide. It might not hear us;
that's beside the point. Lightdark and darklight, two sides
of the same. Spacetime and timespace spinning,
until we break the chains and losefind/findlose ourselves
back in that place that was, before the beginning.

The Song of the Wilderness Wanderer (lyrics)

The path I walk is a path of discovery,
Seeking the wild places of my soul;
The path I walk is a path of recovery,
Learning to find the Love that makes me whole.
With open eyes and ears I wander the wilderness,
Finding the stories of every living thing:
Encountering each tree, each flower, each animal,
Letting them tell me the messages they bring.

Not for me familiar haunts, not for me the tame,
Not for me security, with every day the same,
Not for me the comfort of a place that I call home:
Take me to the wild lands, and set me free to roam!

The path I walk is a path of community,
All of us here connected at the heart;
The path I walk brings a new opportunity,
Open me up, let transformation start!
With open eyes and ears I wander the wilderness,
Where rabbits run, and where the squirrels play:
Remembering that I am only a traveller,
One of the many who walk this ancient way.

The path I walk is a path that is waking me,
Stung by the nettle, scratched by twig and thorn;
The path I walk, I don't know where it's taking me,
All that I know is new dreams are being born.
With open eyes and ears I wander the wilderness,
Losing myself till I find the one who knows;
Conversing with the rocks, the springs and the sacred earth,
Singing as one with a Love that only grows!

PASSION

For Love, Or Not At All (lyrics)

I will do it just because it sets my heart on fire,
I will do it just because it's my spirit's deep desire,
I will do it just because I have heard that inner call:
I will do it for Love, or not at all!

Not because of habit, not because I feel I should,
Not because, if I don't, you'll say that I'm no good;
Not because I'm under pressure,
not because I want the fame,
Not because I need the money,
or fans to shout my name,
Not because everyone else is doing it,
not just because I can,
Not because I think I have to prove to you who I am...

I will link it to the songs my heart still yearns to sing,
I will link it to the joy my soul's true work can bring,
I will link it to the dream that is always burning bright,
I will do it because it feels so right!

I will do it now because Love won't let me refuse,
For my hands are just the tools that Spirit wants to use,
I will do it so that through me, the light of Love will shine,
I will do it because this work is mine!

I will do it just because I have heard that inner call:
I will do it for Love, or not at all!

DISCLAIMER: The author accepts no liability for the consequences of taking this song literally. (I tried it for a few years and ended up with £37,000 worth of debt. I still stand by the principle of doing things for love wherever possible, but money is useful too...)

SOLIDARITY

Songs of the Gathering I: The Call to the Gathering

Come to our gathering, come to the circle,
Come with your fears and we'll turn them to song;
Come with your joy, with your grief, with your gratitude:
Come to the circle: together we're strong.

Come as you are now, and come as you long to be,
Come to this space at your best and your worst,
Come as the person you thought it was wrong to be:
Nothing is wrong when you put your soul first.

Come to our gathering, come to the circle...
Come with your fears and we'll turn them to song;
Come with your joy, with your grief, with your gratitude:
Come to the circle: together we're strong.

Come with your visions, the bold and the wild ones,
Come with that dream that's too big to achieve,
Come and give heart to the meek and the mild ones:
When we're together, we learn to believe.

Come to our gathering, come to the circle...
Come with your fears and we'll turn them to song;
Come with your joy, with your grief, with your gratitude:
Come to the circle: together we're strong.

Come with the song you've been yearning to sing to us,
Share the new hope that's already begun;
Come with the talents and gifts that you bring to us,
Come with the Love that unites us as one.

Come to our gathering, come to the circle...
Come with your fears and we'll turn them to song;
Come with your joy, with your grief, with your gratitude:
Come to the circle: together we're strong.

Songs of the Gathering II: The Circle of Talking

Before you sing, listen to my soul,
and understand the things it yearns for;
Don't speak yet, but look into my eyes,
and see the dreams my spirit burns for;
Our song's our bond, a cord that binds us:
Opens our eyes, and thus reminds us
who we are, where we're from,
and what we've buried deep within:
It lifts us up, and brings us hope,
and gives us somewhere to begin.

Listen, then, listen well,
hear our words and what is left unsaid here,
Through these tales that we tell,
fear dissolves and there is love instead here...

So we rise from the dust,
Know we're safe enough to break the silence,
Learn to hope, learn to trust,
Join together, heal the wounds of violence,
Listen well and enter in, as we begin to remember...

Before I spoke, I listened to your soul,
and heard how deeply we're connected
Knowing this, I looked into your eyes,
and saw my secret dreams reflected...
Our song's our strength, our inmost healing:
Waking us up and thus revealing
who we are, where we're from,
and all the gifts that we've received:
the sacred truths about ourselves
that we've forgotten we believed.

Listen, then, listen well,
hear our words and what is left unsaid here,
Through these tales that we tell,
fear dissolves and there is love instead here...
So we rise from the dust,
Know we're safe enough to break the silence,
Learn to hope, learn to trust,
Join together, heal the wounds of violence,
Listen well and enter in, as we begin to remember...

Welcome, friends, and listen to our souls,
and know it's true the Flame burns bright now;
Welcome, friends, and look into our eyes,
and let our song set hearts alight now!

Our song's our hope, our light returning,
As we unite, and keep on learning
who we are, where we're from,
and all the Love that we have known...
the precious Love reminding us
that we will never be alone.

Songs of the Gathering III: The Circle of Listening

Listen again as you listened before,
Though you're lonely and hesitant, lost and unsure;
Listen again as you did from the start,
Not to the words of our mouths, but the songs of your heart.

Listen and feel, O listen and see,
All that you are now and all you can be;
Listen and see, O listen and feel,
All that's illusion and all that is real;
When we enter the Silence, we heal.

Enter the Silence that speaks to your soul,
Where the sore place is soothed and the broken made whole;
Enter the Silence and maybe you'll know
Some of the secrets of Light you forgot long ago.

Listen and feel, O listen and see,
All that you are now and all you can be;
Listen and see, O listen and feel,
All that's illusion and all that is real;
When we enter the Silence, we heal.

Open your heart to the Silence within,
Where old dreams come to die, and let new ones begin;
Open your heart to the love it can hold,
Till inspiration descends and the mysteries unfold.

Listen and feel, O listen and see,
All that you are now and all you can be;
Listen and see, O listen and feel,
All that's illusion and all that is real;
When we enter the Silence, we heal.

Songs of the Gathering IV: The Circle of Co-Creating

Let me create with you,
show the world something new,
Teach me to listen and teach me to see;
Rise from the source within,
where all my dreams begin,
Be as a fountain that's flowing in me.
Send me a story my soul understands,
Bring it to life through the work of my hands!

Let me create with you,
change me to someone new,
Transform the anger and fear in my heart:
Spiritual alchemy,
setting my power free,
Take each emotion and turn it to art.
Send me a story my soul understands,
Bring it to life through the work of my hands!

Let us create with you,
take us to somewhere new,
Lead us to places we've not seen before,
And when we hide our light,
please keep us burning bright,
Gently remind us that we can be more.

Send us a story each soul understands,
Bring it to life through the work of our hands!

Songs of the Gathering V: Circle Closing Song

Sacred space is where we are,
Sacred time is here and now;
Bound together, near or far,
As we reconfirm our vow...
Fire, water, earth and air,
Where we are, Deep Mystery's there.

Hand in hand, joined as one,
As we leave, we know the work's begun...
Heart to heart, hand in hand,
Reconnecting with the Sacred Land.
Close the circle, each departs,
Let the circle be unbroken in our hearts!

Golden sun and silver moon,
Keepers of the day and night,
Sing to us your haunting tune,
Balancing the dark and light...

Earth below us, sky above,
Teach us songs of timeless love.

Hand in hand, joined as one,
As we leave, we know the work's begun...
Heart to heart, hand in hand,
Reconnecting with the Sacred Land.
Close the circle, each departs,
Let the circle be unbroken in our hearts!

Seasons come and seasons go,
So the wheel of life must turn;
Let our daily actions show
All the mysteries that we learn.
Systems of oppression fall:
With these hands, we'll change it all!

Hand in hand, joined as one,
As we leave, we know the work's begun...
Heart to heart, hand in hand,
Reconnecting with the Sacred Land.
Close the circle, each departs,
Let the circle be unbroken in our hearts!

ABOUT SONGWORK

I use the term 'Songwork' to refer to a process of using songs to hold space for different types of human interactions. This process, which I also call the 'TLC Gathering', can help to create a sense of solidarity and mutual empathy that provides a strong foundation for difficult conversations.

Songwork can be a powerful tool for building collective well-being and resilience, especially when used in support groups or faith communities that are trying to unpack colonial legacies of racism, homophobia, misogyny, and transphobia. I've used it with groups of friends at home, with a group of colleagues at work, in public workshops, at conferences, and even as part of an Anglican church service to celebrate Pride month. More recently, I've also started trying it out in environmental education and climate activism contexts, as a strategy for moving beyond the cycles of denial and despair that get in the way of radical action.

It's also possible to do Songwork through online video calling platforms like Zoom, although unfortunately, this technology has not yet developed to a point at which everyone can sing together at the same time. The workaround is to keep everyone muted except the facilitator, so that the individual participants can hear only the facilitator and themselves. This is less fun for the facilitator, who's left feeling as though they're singing to an empty room! But the online method has the advantage of enabling participation by people who are in different continents, countries, and time zones.

The acronym 'TLC' stands for Tender Loving Care, as it does in everyday language; but it also stands for the three circles of *Talking, Listening, and Co-Creating*, each introduced by its respective song:

- **The Circle of Talking** builds on traditions common to many parts of the world: a 'talking stick' (or bowl or other object) is passed around the circle and people take it in turns to speak with honesty and sensitivity about something personal. I like to use 'joy, grief, or gratitude' as a prompt to help people get to a deeper level of vulnerability, rather than talking about their social roles or what they're working on. Only the person holding the object is allowed to talk, which reduces people's innate tendency to jump in with advice or start making comparisons with their experience.
- **The Circle of Listening** is a time of silence in which participants reflect on what has just been shared and listen to their own inner wisdom. Depending on the context, this might be framed as `meditation', `connecting with the higher Self', or 'waiting on the Spirit' – or just giving people a quiet space to write, draw, or doodle. This may feel quite uncomfortable at first, especially for people who are not used to this type of practice, and there is nothing wrong with limiting it to 5-10 minutes initially.
- **The Circle of Co-Creating** is a process of making something together. What is co-created will depend very much on the group and its purpose. It could be as simple as

a conversation in which everyone shares what came up for them during the 'Listening' time - building solidarity, shared identity, and a sense of interconnectedness. It might be a vision, plan, or strategy. It could even be a collective artwork, such as a collage made from everyone's individual drawings, or a blanket in which everyone knits a square.

At the end of the gathering, the Circle Closing Song is sung. At this point, most groups that are meeting in person like to share food and drink - a potluck approach often works well, if everyone's dietary needs are considered.

'But I Can't Sing!'

When I talk about songwork to people in England for the first time, I can almost guarantee that at least three-quarters of them will respond with a comment about their inability to sing. It's a sad reflection on the state of music education in this country, at least in earlier generations, that so many people hold this belief. Televised singing competitions, in which people's voices are publicly judged and often ridiculed, have probably not helped either. It's nearly always untrue anyway - anyone who can speak can almost certainly sing! But one of the hardest things to convey about songwork, to people who haven't experienced it, is how little attention is paid to the pitch or tone of anyone's voice. It isn't a choir rehearsal or a performance: it's a way of working *with* song to achieve shared goals, rather than treating the song as an end in itself.

Songwork is about being in the moment, resisting any urge to judge yourself or anyone else, absorbing the meanings of the lyrics, and connecting with other people through sound.

Having said all that, if confidence is a real issue for anyone, the facilitator should never pressure them to sing aloud. They can be encouraged to sing very quietly, or hum along, or just listen until they forget to be nervous and find themselves joining in.

A note on copyright (or the lack of it!)

These songs are for you. They're non-copyrighted and have been shared under a more open arrangement called a Creative Commons license. This also applies to all the other songs and poems in this book.

You're allowed, and in fact positively encouraged, to make copies and share them with friends. You can screenshot them, photocopy the pages, type them out, post them on your social media, set them to music, distribute scores, record yourselves singing them – all completely free of charge. You can even change the lyrics (e.g., if certain words don't work well in your context) or translate them into other languages, and then share the modified versions. There are only three conditions:

- You should **credit the original author**, using the wording 'By Ash Brockwell, 2022. Shared under Creative Commons Attribution-NonCommercial-ShareAlike (CC-BY-NC-SA) 4.0 International Licence. Some rights reserved.'
- The licence only extends to **non-commercial use**, which means that you're not making money from the use of the songs. If you would like to make commercial recordings or give ticketed performances, please get in touch via the publisher's website to negotiate a fair arrangement for fees or royalties.
- If you make changes and share a modified version, you should **clearly indicate what has been changed**. If you

share a translation, it must be accompanied by the original English version. New versions must be shared under the same terms as the original, with the wording 'Original version by Ash Brockwell, 2022; this version by [Author Name], [Date].

For more information on these T&Cs, please visit: https://creativecommons.org/licenses/by-nc-sa/4.0/

Where can I find the music, or a recording of the songs?

Currently, nowhere – sorry! At the time of publication, I'm working on a plan to record the Songs of the Gathering and make them publicly available - alongside another song cycle, called *Nineteen Songs of Remembering*, which will be published in a forthcoming book. I'm also working on getting them transcribed as musical scores so that they can be shared more easily with people who know how to read music.

If there's enough demand, I would be open to offering a short course for facilitators. In the meantime, the best way to learn the original tunes is to contact me via the publisher's website and ask if there are any upcoming online songwork gatherings – or set up a group and invite me to join online!

An even better option is to set the lyrics to your own tunes. There's nothing particularly special or sacred about the original tunes – they're just the ones that 'came through' for me, at a particular time and in a particular place. Making up your own tunes enables you to use a style of music that works for you and your community, customise the lyrics to fit your local context, and even translate them if you want to.

I'd love to receive copies of any recordings you make (please don't forget to licence them under the same terms as the original lyrics). Maybe over time, we can build a digital archive of recordings in different languages and styles – a true 'creative commons'!

ACKNOWLEDGEMENTS

First and foremost, I want to acknowledge the lands I walk on, and have walked on in this lifetime. Many of the songs in this book 'came through' – by which I mean that they arrived in my mind as fully formed songs, as unlikely as that may seem – while I was walking in the New Forest in southern England between 2015 and 2018. Other places that have contributed to making me who I am today include Bursledon, Oxford (especially Christ Church Meadow, Port Meadow, and the Treacle Well at Binsey), Arusha, Monduli (especially Eluwai), Mount Kilimanjaro, Canterbury, Avebury, Glastonbury (especially Chalice Well and Bride's Mound), and most recently Mile End Park, Tower Hamlets Cemetery Park, and the north Cornish coast. Special thanks to all the people, known and unknown, who protect these magical places.

Words can't express my gratitude to all the people who have kept me alive and writing. To my mum and my daughters. To my beloved friend, Pinku, still meecey after all these years and all those Aawksford degrees: your WhatsApp messages enrich and brighten my life more than you'll ever know. One of these days we'll meet again in person, and it'll be as though we'd never been apart. May you never forget that day by the river in Oxford - and may the unending birthday saga never end! Happy birthday (again)!

To my creative muses, my unrequited loves, Loni and Astara. Loving you nearly killed me, but I'm mostly over it now. In any case, I got a lot of poetic inspiration out of it. I hope you never read this: it would be extremely embarrassing.

To everyone who has ever been part of my song circles, and especially Kestral, whom I also want to thank for being my constant supporter, my writing buddy, my fellow activist, and often my lifeline. I hope one day you realise how awesome you really are. And to Compton, who already knows it very well: thanks for being fluffy and adorable.

To Chrissie Chevasutt, author of *Heaven Come Down*: thanks for being a wonderful role model, pastor, and friend. I'm finally getting my ass in gear and sharing all this super scary vulnerable emotional stuff because you did it first, and I've seen for myself how life-saving that can be.

To Nila: thanks for all the home-cooked meals, garden time, and encouragement. I hope you make the space to write your own book one day - it deserves a movie! To Moriah Ama Hope, whose nascent book *Labyrinth: My Journey to Belonging* has been an ongoing source of inspiration and encouragement - and to Astrid, for accompanying me on the quest for real-life labyrinths and bringing me back to Goddess House. To whoever carved the Rocky Valley labyrinths, whether you were a Bronze Age shaman or a Victorian eccentric: you rock.

To all the *TransVerse* and *TV2* crew, and especially to Dalton Harrison, author of *The Boy Behind the Wall*: mate, you're an inspiration, and I wouldn't be where I am without you. I know you say that to me a lot, but I'm throwing it right back at you now. Hope you're getting on with the sequel. And to Paula and Chrissie (the other Chrissie in my life): thanks for making me believe in love again after heartbreak had made me all cynical.

Get that book written as soon as you can, please – the world needs a trans lesbian love story told in poems!

To Jani Franck, Dave Hubble, Bik, Missy, Ziggy, and the rest of the Art House crew: huge thanks for believing in me and hosting my first exhibition. Love you all. Keep on arting! Dave, you get a bonus thank-you for inviting me to poetry events at the John Hansard Gallery, which inspired some of my favourite poems in this book – *A Lover's Guide to the Electromagnetic Spectrum, Surviving (But Only Just)*, and *The Tarantella of the Plague-Spirits* – and for being a great trans ally. You are awesome and I'm so glad you're recovering well.

To Hannah and the rest of the GHT team: thanks for the opportunity to co-host the 'Write It Out' festival. Thanks also to the participating visual artists (Jack Pudding, Orlando Myxx, Aliya Cambray, Debbie Goatley Birch, and yes, Jani Franck again) for sharing artworks that inspired poems in this book.

To all my former teachers, especially Yvonne Kinsella, Yvonne Castino, and Sheila and Ken Charisse: a huge thank you for believing in me and encouraging me. It might have taken longer than expected, but I finally have a poetry book of my own!

To Tona, badass to the end. Thanks for being brave enough to live your dreams, inspiring me to live mine and get these damn poems out into the world. I think you'd have enjoyed some of them, although you'd definitely have rolled your eyes at others! And to Eve, Andi, Charmaine and Rory: thanks for introducing me to such an unforgettable young woman, and for encouraging everyone you know to #bemoreTona.

To everyone I've forgotten to thank: I apologise. It isn't personal: I'm just getting older, and my memory isn't what it used to be. I still love you, and I'm still grateful.

To all my readers: You are enough. You are valid. You are loved. Thanks for reading to the end.

POSTSCRIPT: TO THE READER

In case you didn't read
the dedication at the beginning of this book
or the acknowledgements at the end
    (and let's face it, who reads
    the dedication at the beginning of a book
    or the acknowledgements at the end
    unless they're either related to the author,
    secretly in love with the author,
    or so vain that they're expecting a mention?)
here it is again.
Your bit of it.

You are enough.
You are valid
You are loved.

You've got this.
Life is a process,
not a product.
It isn't always shiny,
it doesn't always feel good,
and that's OK.
It will be worth it, I promise.

Your voice matters.
Your story matters.
Your words matter.

Write it.
Speak it.
Sing it.

Never give up.

ALSO PUBLISHED BY RECONNECTING RAINBOWS PRESS:

TransVerse, We Won't Be Erased!
Poems and Song Lyrics by Transgender and Non-Binary Writers
Edited by Ash Brockwell, 2019

TransVerse II, No Time For Silence:
Words of Survival, Resilience and Hope
Edited by Ash Brockwell, 2021

The Boy Behind The Wall:
Poems of Imprisonment and Freedom
Dalton Harrison, 2022

Counterweights - poetry collection
Kestral Gaian, 2022

Hidden Lives - a young adult novel
Kestral Gaian, 2022

Forthcoming:

TransVerse III, Transcendence:
Words of Faith, Love and Authenticity

TransVerse IV, The Wait Is Killing Us:
Trans and Non-Binary People Demand Healthcare Justice!

Twenty-Eight: These Are Our Stories
Edited by Kestral Gaian

Sing Back Hope!
Using Songwork to Build Community and Catalyse Change
Ash Brockwell